The Scots Pine

Phil Gates

CAMBRIDGE
UNIVERSITY PRESS

Cambridge Reading

General Editors
Richard Brown and Kate Ruttle

Consultant Editor
Jean Glasberg

PUBLISHED BY THE PRESS SYNDICATE OF THE UNIVERSITY OF CAMBRIDGE
The Pitt Building, Trumpington Street, Cambridge CB2 1RP

CAMBRIDGE UNIVERSITY PRESS
The Edinburgh Building, Cambridge CB2 2RU, United Kingdom
40 West 20th Street, New York, NY 10011-4211, USA
10 Stamford Road, Oakleigh, Melbourne 3166, Australia

First published 1996
Reprinted 1997

Printed in the United Kingdom at the University Press, Cambridge

A catalogue record for this book is available from the British Library

ISBN 0 521 49932 1 paperback

Picture Research: Callie Kendall

Acknowledgements

We are grateful to the following for permission to reproduce photographs:
Front cover, C.H. Gomersall/RSPB Photo Library; *title page*, Crown
copyright/Forest Life Picture Library; 4*t*, 12 (*inset*), 14*t*, 15, 16*tr*, 16*b*, 17*b*,
Phil Gates; 4*b*, Forestry Commission Photographic Library; 6, 17*t*, 20 (*main pic*),
Niall Benvie/Oxford Scientific Films; 7*t*, Isobel Cameron/Forest Life Picture Library;
7*b*, Stephen Downer/Oxford Scientific Films; 8*t*, Laurie Campbell/Natural History
Photographic Agency; 8*b*, R.T. Smith/RSPB Photo Library; 9, W.S. Paton/RSPB
Photo Library; 10 (*main pic*), 11*t*, Chris H. Gomersall/RSPB Photo Library; 11*b*
Michael W. Richards/RSPB Photo Library; 12 (*main pic*), T.C. Middleton/Oxford
Scientific Films; 13*tl*, Nigel Cattlin/Holt Studios International; 13*tr*, P.R. Perfect/
RSPB Photo Library; 13*bl*, M.P.L. Fogden/Oxford Scientific Films; 13*br*, Colin
Carver/RSPB Photo Library; 14*bl*, Forest Life Picture Library; 14 *br*, S.I. Bernard/
Oxford Scientific Films; 16*tl*, 19*b*, Terry Heathcote/Oxford Scientific Films; 18,
Michael Leach/Oxford Scientific Films; 19*t*, Paul Taylor/Oxford Scientific Films;
20 (*inset*), R.J.B. Goodale/ Oxford Scientific Films; 21*t,* Roger Wilmshurst/ RSPB
Photo Library; 21*c*, Tony Tilford/Oxford Scientific Films; 21*b*, Philip J. Newman/
RSPB Photo Library; 22, Michael W. Richards/Oxford Scientific Films
RSPB = Royal Society for the Protection of Birds

Contents

The Scots pine

This pine tree is called a Scots pine.

Pine trees are evergreen trees. The leaves of evergreen trees stay on the branches all through the year. They stay green even in winter.

Most Scots pine trees grow in forests.

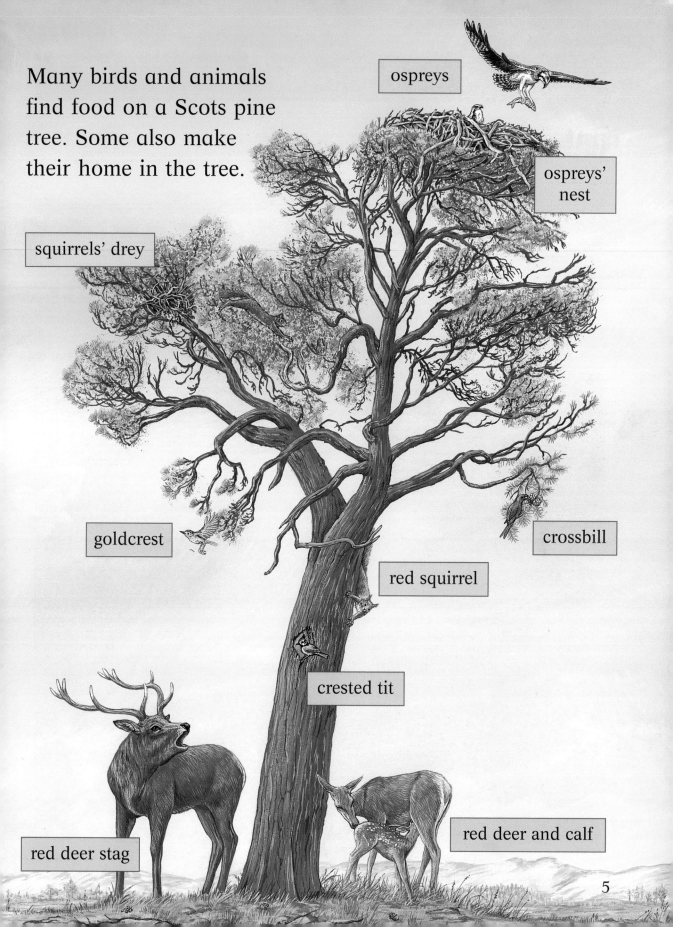

Many birds and animals find food on a Scots pine tree. Some also make their home in the tree.

ospreys

ospreys' nest

squirrels' drey

goldcrest

crossbill

red squirrel

crested tit

red deer and calf

red deer stag

5

Red squirrels

Red squirrels live in pine forests. They make their homes in the branches of Scots pine trees.

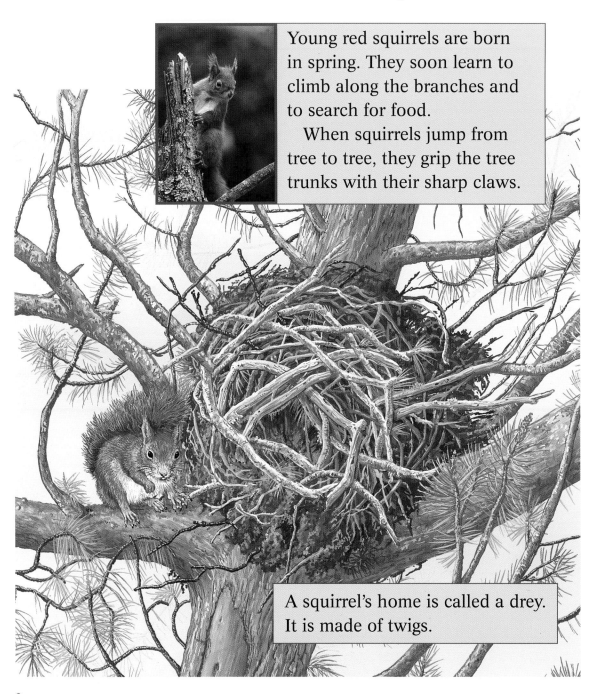

Young red squirrels are born in spring. They soon learn to climb along the branches and to search for food.

When squirrels jump from tree to tree, they grip the tree trunks with their sharp claws.

A squirrel's home is called a drey. It is made of twigs.

New leaves in spring

In spring, new leaves grow on the branches of Scots pine trees. The leaves are soft at first.

Squirrels like to eat the new leaves.

Red deer

Red deer often live in pine forests. They sometimes eat the new leaves of Scots pine trees.

An adult male deer is called a stag. Stags have antlers on their heads.

Every spring, the stag's antlers fall off.

Then the stag grows new antlers. When antlers begin to grow on the stag's head, they have a soft covering called velvet.

The stag rubs the velvet off against the rough bark and spiky branches of a Scots pine.

Ospreys

Ospreys often make their homes high in the branches of tall Scots pine trees. They build their nests from sticks.

The female osprey lays two or three eggs in the nest.

The ospreys feed their chicks with fish which they catch in lakes. They carry the slippery fish home in their sharp claws.

Young ospreys leave the nest when their feathers have grown. They stand on the branches and flap their wings. Soon they will be able to fly and catch fish for themselves.

Pine needles

By summer, the new pine leaves have hardened. They are now very sharp and are called pine needles.

Squirrels and deer do not like to eat these sharp needles. They like to eat the soft, young leaves.

Insects and birds

Lots of different insects eat pine needles. Birds come to the pine trees to catch the insects.

Small insects, like greenfly, feed on pine needles.

Goldcrests eat the insects.

Caterpillars of pine hawkmoths also eat pine needles.

Crested tits eat caterpillars and other small insects.

Pine cones

Pine trees grow from seeds.
The seeds grow inside a cone.

1

The seeds are inside a female cone, which is small and soft at first.

2

These are male cones. Male cones make pollen, which is like a yellow dust.

3

The pollen blows in the wind. When it lands on a female cone, the cone begins to grow.

The male cones fall off the tree after their pollen has gone.

When the female cones are one year old, they are long, green and shiny.

When the female cones are two years old, they are dry, brown and hard. The seeds inside them are now fully grown.

15

1

On warm, sunny days the hard, female cones open. Then the seeds fall out of the cones and are blown away by the wind.

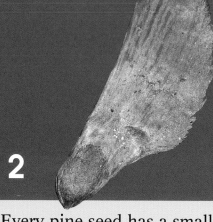

2

Every pine seed has a small wing which makes the seed spin around in the wind.

3

When a seed lands on the ground, a tiny root begins to grow.

After a few weeks, spiky leaves begin to grow.

4

The young pine tree
grows towards the light.

Try this

If you can find a
pine cone, leave it
on the window-
ledge outside.

On warm, sunny days the cone
will open. On cold, wet days it
will close.

Seeds as food

Some seeds do not grow into new trees because they are eaten by birds and animals.

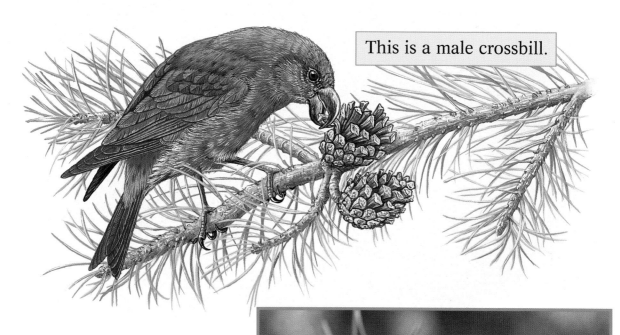

This is a male crossbill.

Crossbills like to eat pine seeds. Their scissor-shaped beaks can reach the seeds that are hidden between the scales of pine cones.

This is a female crossbill.

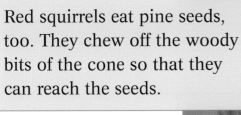

Red squirrels eat pine seeds, too. They chew off the woody bits of the cone so that they can reach the seeds.

It is easy to see where a squirrel has been eating cones. The squirrel leaves untidy piles of chewed cones everywhere.

Autumn in the forest

In autumn, ospreys fly to Africa to find a warmer home for the winter.

All the animals that stay behind in the forest
must find food before winter comes.

Squirrels search for cones in the highest branches of Scots pine trees.

Crossbills search for pine seeds.

Crested tits search for insects.

Winter in the forest

When winter comes, the branches of the Scots pine trees are often covered with snow.

Squirrels do not like the cold, so they stay in their dreys for most of the winter. They curl up in their dreys and wrap their tails around themselves to keep warm.

Glossary

antlers

Antlers are the horns which grow on a stag's head. They look like the branches of a tree.

cones

See pine cones.

drey

A *drey* is the home of a squirrel. It is made of twigs.

evergreen

An *evergreen* tree has green leaves on its branches all through the year.

needles

See pine needles.

pine cones

Seeds grow inside female *pine cones*. There are often cones lying on the ground near a pine tree.

pine needles

The hard, sharp leaves of a pine tree are called *pine needles*.

pollen

Pollen is a yellow dust made in male pine cones. When pollen is blown onto female pine cones, the seeds inside the cones start to grow.

scales

Scales are the small, hard parts on the outside of a female pine cone. The scales protect the seeds that are inside the cone.

stag

A *stag* is an adult male deer.

velvet

The soft skin which covers a stag's new antlers is called *velvet*.

Index

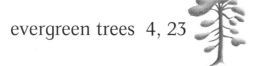